THE WOMB

-Planned Parenthood God's Way-

Mia White

Dedicated to:

The man God gave me,
with whom I share the journey of surrender.

Introduction   p. 1

Chapter One
My Journey of Surrender   p. 3

Chapter Two
The Womb and the Scriptures   p. 13

Chapter Three
What Happened to the Scriptural
Paradigm?   p. 25

Chapter Four
A Generation Needing to be Born   p. 37

Chapter Five
Examining Mind-sets that Oppose
the Open Womb   p. 51

Chapter Six
Examining Fears Concerning
the Open Womb   p. 67

Conclusion   p. 91

Appendix I
A Closed, Weak or Deprived Womb   i

Appendix II
Beyond Abortion   vii

Acknowledgements

Thank you for seeing the potential
of the manuscript I handed you,
dear friend and editor, Mahreen Shamim.
Your encouragement and support became my beacon!

Thank you, Mrs. Nancy Campbell,
for being such an inspiration to me and so many!
Your helpfulness in completing this book was invaluable.

Thank you, to the mothers that inspire me
to be courageous on my journey by their own example.
Geke, and Susan, I admire you!

Thank you, to the friends who have loved our big, messy, family
through the years, and never condemned.
There are so many of you!

Thank you, to each arrow the Lord placed in our quiver;
for the forgiveness and acceptance you give me
on my journey with motherhood.
You are fiercely awesome beyond description!

Endorsements

There are books that entertain, and books that bring transformational change. I like this book because it falls into the latter category by challenging us to examine assumptions current western culture makes about children and family. It does what a good teacher would: It informs, it provokes, and it asks powerful questions. I know this author well. Mia is a gifted musician, a multi-talented woman, and amazing mother. Our children are friends. She's a trusted voice, and in this volume, she speaks honestly of her journey of discovery on the issue of the womb. It is a topic that we all have an opinion on, either consciously or unconsciously. Weaving personal narrative with historical context and scriptural wisdom, Mia causes us to look with heaven's eyes at the subject of children and family. This is a book to read, savor, and process personally and with your spouse or other close friends. It just might change your heart and mind and change the trajectory of your life and the legacy you leave behind. I think these themes resonate in my heart as I read Mia's journey, because they echo much of the personal journey my wife and I have taken on this subject as well. The message at the core of this book is an urgent wake-up call to the Church, to think past the immediate and on to long-term legacy and impact. It is a needed message.

Robert Rummage
Pastor of Prayer, Elder
MorningStar Fellowship Church, Fort Mill SC

The Womb is an urgent message from Mia White. In this book, she shares her own personal journey of getting married and choosing to close her womb to God, to surrendering it soon after as she learned of His plans for nations and generations. She gives a prophetic call to move past our mindsets, fears and culture, to embrace a supernatural life of obedience to God by opening our hearts to birth a mighty generation. She supports her ideas in a theologically balanced way, explaining from Scripture that the womb is a gift, in combination with the many other gifts given to a Proverbs 31 woman. She deeply investigates our culture, which consistently through the ages either aborts or prevents life from entering the womb. Mia insightfully shows us the bigger picture of what the world desperately needs now: For us to birth children to radically bring the Kingdom to all spheres of their generation; to be the problem-solvers, the God-creatives, and the righteous salt and light to the nations. I highly recommend reading this book and searching your own heart to see what God would have you do with this call. God is raising up an end-time army of champions that will shape and change the world as we know it, through the many families who answer this call for their lives!

Amy Rummage
Elder at MorningStar Fellowship Church, Fort Mill SC
Mother of 8 mighty warriors

"Before I formed you in the womb I knew you,
before you were born I set you apart." (Jeremiah 1:5)

"All the days ordained for me were written in your book
before one of them came to be." (Psalm 139:16)

INTRODUCTION

Years ago, God powerfully spoke these words in my spirit: *"You think in terms of me, mine, and the here and now. I think in terms of nations and generations."* That challenging statement is the foundational message of this book. In fact, if we understood the practical implications of it, I would need to write no further.

Typing the pages you are now holding requires sharing a most personal area of my life's journey with you. In doing so, I invite you to venture to that same vulnerable place within yourselves, and I do it very cautiously. I'm talking about the most sacred space of our hearts, where *true surrender* happens. This kind of surrender may involve discomfort and sacrifice, but it also assuredly fills our lives with the thrill and fulfillment of radical abandonment to Jesus.

I pray this book will excite you about the potential impact your family can have in our world. May your paradigm be stretched by a personal revelation of God's concern, not only for individuals; but for communities and nations. May you see that the decisions we make in our homes inevitably affect the bigger picture of God's Kingdom expanding on earth. So... here in these pages come age old truths revisited, as well as a prophetic call to action. As you read on, I pray you get a glimpse of how your family's destiny and best adventure is related to the *gift of the womb*.

CHAPTER ONE
MY JOURNEY OF SURRENDER

When I entered marriage and family-building at the age of 23, I had no idea what I was embarking upon. I was fresh out of spending 15 years of my life educated in various schools, but nothing thus far had prepared me for the feat of being a wife and mother. Being raised in Europe, I took pride in my training to question and analyze everything around me. But challenging the status quo on motherhood and family were not within my sight.

Even though I grew up in a church context, I don't remember ever hearing teachings on God's view on family. What I did learn in church was that relationship struggles were to be kept out of sight, so that a paradigm based on an unrealistic ideal of family could be maintained. As a result, no one would know anything was the matter, until a household crumbled. Both shame and rejection would follow from those still maintaining a facade. I realized that behind the pretense were plenty of examples of what I did *not* want my newly started home to be like. I could only find a few authentic cases where family represented something safe and beautiful.

My own family background was wrecked with multiple traumas. When my father left us after years of marital struggle, so did my last bit of security and my understanding of unconditional love. From a young age, family to me became equated with chaos and loneliness. As an adult, I came to the realization that even my view of womanhood and motherhood was greatly distorted from the time my father left us. My mother, who had experienced personality-altering brain trauma due to a car accident, had to manage the best she could as the single provider for me and my siblings. Always battling depression, as heart wrenching events kept being launched our way, she became a workaholic with a focus on survival and protecting her heart from more hurt.

I feel no resentment as I look back at how circumstances prevented my mother from being available for my needs as a child. On the contrary, I'm so grateful that we somehow lived through those years. We did, however, come away with some messed up life paradigms, and plenty of need for inner healing. I believe that hurting people attract other hurting people. The man who attracted my attention and became my Prince Charming thus came lugging along his own share of family-paradigm distortions. Despite all the baggage we both had, we at least knew that we married each other in obedience to God's guidance. We were still young in the understanding of how far reaching His guidance really is though, and how He wants our surrender *in all things*.

When it came to making plans for children, my husband and I simply operated from the social cues of our time, as we lacked alternative paradigms. The rational way of thinking that permeated both church and society went something like this: "A couple needs time to focus on their marriage and careers before having children. After a few years, when they have had freedom and fun, and saved up enough money for the expense of raising a family, they can try for a baby. A couple of years after their first child they may try for a second. Hopefully, they now have a boy and a girl. This is the recipe for family bliss."

When I got pregnant one month after our wedding day, as we had just started our life as missionaries in Africa, we were stunned. Faced with this surprise the demise of our "perfect-family-plan" began. As we rearranged our life and returned to Europe for the birth our daughter, the crumbling of many of our unrealistic expectations continued. To say that motherhood was harder than I fathomed is an understatement. I was overwhelmed by the changes in my life. What would being someone else's 24-7 caregiver mean for me? What would happen to my self-fulfillment, rest, and comfort? How would the loss of independence affect my career, ministry, and social life?

Since I'm a determined person, I decided to continue my life as if nothing had changed after the baby was born, simply adding her as an attachment to my currently full and busy life. It didn't take long before I ended up with a stressed infant who couldn't sleep due to overstimulation. And of course, I was beyond exhausted and had to pause and reconsider my priorities. I desperately wish I had been taught life skills for this season in my life.

Less than a year later, as I stopped nursing our first baby Ronya, we were further jolted by the discovery of a second pregnancy. People began to roll their eyes at our apparent ignorance as to how to prevent these surprises.

Nine months later, our son was born. It quickly became evident that the transition to parent two children was almost as hard as becoming a mother in the first place. Now we had to learn to juggle the needs of two little ones. But at least we weren't outnumbered. Since we had a boy and a girl we were ready to put an end to bombshell pregnancies, and find "family bliss."

My husband and I trudged along in a shaky marriage, busy with work and ministry. After about two years, circumstances arose that resulted in us moving from Europe to my husband's home country, Bermuda. Little did I know what awaited us there. Had God shown me beforehand I'm sure I would have laughed like Sarah in the Bible. But instead of revealing His plans before we were ready, He worked secretly, in the hiddenness of our hearts.

At this point in our marriage, we were growing in the understanding of living a supernatural life of faith. But, we had never thought to apply faith to our current ideas of family planning. Soon, God began to prepare us for deeper levels of abandonment to Him, and a broader paradigm for our family. After all, we had given our hearts to the Lord. We had professed our complete surrender many times, albeit not understanding the ramifications of such a yielding. We had prayed for His *perfect* will for our lives, and meant it. Now came the "cash-in" of these confessions.

On a seemingly normal day, a friend came to our house and announced that he believed God had more children to give our family. Since the delivery of my son, I only thought about my womb if I forgot to take my birth-control-pill. Strangely enough, the friend's words, like an arrow, profoundly pierced my heart. It dawned on me right then, that I never once asked for God's opinion on the matter of my womb and how many children He might desire for us to have. It was as if I had unknowingly held a part of my heart from Him. Years earlier, I had decided to live a life of *faith*. To me, that meant that if I found myself making decisions based on *fear*, I had to re-evaluate and surrender to God. I recognized that my choice to close my womb to more children was a fear-filled decision.

Fast-forward eighteen years of mountains and valleys; six more children and many adventures later, I marvel at the course my life took. Not much turned out the way I expected. As I sacrificed some things in the process, and became a homemaker and mother of eight, I discovered I did not want it any other way.

I don't always understand why God took me on this route. It wasn't an easy adjustment at first. I remember feeling such frustration as I read stories about mothers of other big families. What was so hard for me seemed easy for them. Did they truly keep a clean house, cook healthy food (some would grow their own!), raise obedient children who loved God, and greet their husbands with a smile each night? Was this idyllic picture what I had to produce on my own journey? If so, I felt I could never qualify.

As you read my story, I hope you do not glorify my life the way I did when I looked at the lives of other mothers. Nobody benefits from a book that paints a picture of an idealistic unreachable goal, seemingly reserved for a select few. Just like most of us enter marriage with brokenness and unhealed pain from the past, we continue experiencing difficult times on our journey of family building. This is life.

This book doesn't allow much space for me to talk extensively about my times of struggle, failure, depression, sickness, and even disaster within our family. But they were certainly there. I confess that the hardest thing to face, throughout the various struggles, has been *myself*. I tell people that I confidently believed that I was a nice person, until I had children. It is uncanny how little ones bring out the ugliest sides of who we are and make us face the reality of our brokenness. Feeling overwhelmed often, and learning about grace even more, has become a way of life for me.

My thinking on motherhood and family planning is obviously radically different today than when I first got married. The change in me didn't happen over-night, and it didn't come without having to deal with contention in my heart. But, over time, I finally questioned the societal paradigms around me. Because of my journey into the meaning of motherhood, I see the significance and value of a single life and a single family more clearly. I see that we are each influencers of an important larger picture of nations, generations, and God's Kingdom expanding in the earth. These are the kinds of insights I want to share with you.

To facilitate you in thinking deeper about your own beliefs surrounding family planning, I am ending each chapter with some questions. Use these questions to promote dialogue between you and God, your spouse, and even other parents if you like. Also, because the Scriptures have more power than my words, I encourage you to also prayerfully read the Bible verses included in the book.

"Do not conform to the pattern of this world,
but be transformed by the renewing
of your mind.
Then you will be able to test and approve
what God's will is—
his good, pleasing and perfect will."
(Romans 12:2)

"I know the plans I have for you,
declares the LORD,
plans to prosper you and not to harm you,
plans to give you hope and a future."
(Jeremiah 29:11)

QUESTIONS

1. How would you describe your present thinking/paradigm concerning family planning?

2. How much of your answer to question number one are conclusions from seeking God's heart? How much became yours "by default" through upbringing, media exposure, and education?

3. If you have decided to close your womb to more children, what are your reasons for this decision? What factors would cause you to reevaluate this decision?

CHAPTER TWO
THE WOMB AND THE SCRIPTURES

I assume that if you are still holding this book in your hands, and have not put it down yet, you are interested in knowing what God's word says about family planning. In this chapter, we look at several Scriptural principles related to the womb. These truths are like treasures waiting to be unearthed. As my eyes opened to these Scriptures I realized my need to pursue an understanding of how to apply them to my life. My commitment to the Bible, and my faith in it being true and applicable to every age, gave me no option but to reshape my view of family.

Principle One: Welcoming the Fruit of the Womb is an Act of Obedience

In Genesis chapter one, we discover that the first commandment ever given to man concerns the womb.

> *"God blessed them and said to them,*
> *'Be fruitful and increase in number.'"* **(Genesis 1:28)**

This verse hides more than instructions for us to follow. It contains a mind-stretching privilege. God decided to share the process of creating *life* with us. This is a wild thought! Out of the mysterious unity between a man and woman comes a *brand-new creation*. The human part is simple; enjoy the pleasure of sexual unity and *allow* the miracle to happen. God Himself brings it to completion, when *He* sees fit. This is what the first mother, Eve, exclaimed as she gave birth:

> *"With the help of the Lord I have brought forth a man."*
> **(Genesis 4:1)**

Principle Two: Receiving the Fruit of the Womb is a Blessing and Privilege

When God looked at the work of His hands, He declared that the order of creation was *good*. For generations, people marveled at the blessing God bestowed upon man in allowing us to partake in the birthing of life. In fact, the Biblical paradigm asserts that the *more* fruitful a woman was, the more she was deemed favored by God. The *more* children around a man's table, the more his household was considered blessed.

> *"Your wife will be like a fruitful vine within your house;*
> *your sons will be like olive shoots around your table.*
> *Thus is the man blessed who fears the LORD."*
> **(Psalm 128:3-4)**

> *"Sons are a heritage from the LORD,*
> *children a reward from him.*

Like arrows in the hands of a warrior
are sons born in one's youth.
Blessed is the man whose quiver is full of them."
(Psalm 127:3-5)

Whenever God made covenants and gave promises of prospering His people, they continuously involved references to *countless seed, fruitful wombs,* and *multiplying.* Here are some examples:

"I am going to make you fruitful
and will increase your numbers.
I will make you a community of peoples,
and I will give this land
as an everlasting possession
to your descendants after you." **(Genesis 48:4)**

"...because of the Almighty, who blesses you
with blessings of the heavens above,
blessings of the deep that lies below,
blessings of the breast and womb." **(Genesis 49:25)**

"The LORD will grant you abundant prosperity—
in the fruit of your womb, the young of your livestock, and the
crops of your ground—
in the land he swore to your forefathers to give you."
(Deuteronomy 28:11)

Principle Three: A Barren/Closed Womb is a Dishonor

Related to the previous principle, we find that a closed or barren womb was a disgrace in Bible times. For years I considered myself blessed when my womb was empty, whereas in the culture of the Scriptures not conceiving was considered a punishment or curse.

> *"...she became pregnant and gave birth to a son*
> *and said, 'God has taken away my disgrace.'"*
> **(Genesis 30:23)**

> *"Then Abraham prayed to God,*
> *and God healed Abimelech,*
> *his wife and his slave girls*
> *so they could have children again,*
> *for the LORD had closed up every womb*
> *in Abimelech's household*
> *because of Abraham's wife Sarah."* **(Genesis 20:17-18)**

Principle Four: God Decides Over the Fruitfulness of Each Womb

This principle is perhaps the one that reaches the furthest into our personal place of surrender. As human beings, we typically like to feel empowered. Relinquishing control is a big deal to most of us. When it comes to releasing control of the womb in particular, all kinds of fears normally arise concerning bills, mortgages, careers, stress, and loss of freedom.

In the Bible, where life revolved around the cycle of fertility and multi-generational families lived together, women found great purpose and joy in birthing and raising children. The fact that God was the one deciding when a womb opened or closed was a given. When there was barrenness, the women knew Who to cry out to for breakthrough. When a womb was blessed with a child, they knew Who to thank and give credit to: The Creator.

"Then God remembered Rachel;
he listened to her and opened her womb."
(Genesis 30:22)

"But to Hannah he gave a double portion
because he loved her,
and the LORD had closed her womb." **(1 Samuel 1:5)**

"When the LORD saw that Leah was not loved,
he opened her womb, but Rachel was barren."
(Genesis 29:31)

Principle Five: The Enemy Opposes God's Ideals and Commands, Including Those Surrounding the Womb

Ever since the Garden of Eden, Satan's objective is to cause us to question God's authority in every matter.

> *"Now the serpent was more crafty*
> *than any of the wild animals the LORD God had made.*
> *He said to the woman,*
> *'Did God really say...?'"* (Genesis 3:1)

Did God really know what He was asking of us when He set the order of creation in place? Perhaps there is a better way than multiplying people whenever God sees fit? Perhaps we will be happier if we take charge ourselves? If we seek to control our own lives God lets us. But as in the Garden of Eden, going our own way has consequences. The effects of the trend to control and close wombs will be discussed more in upcoming chapters. We will also look at how vehemently our enemy goes after the unborn, in order to stall and prevent God's purposes being fulfilled through children on the earth.

> *"Your enemy the devil prowls around like a roaring lion*
> *looking for someone to devour."* (1 Peter 5:8)

Principle Six: The Order of Creation is God's Ideal, Even Under the "New Covenant"

The reason for including this Biblical Principle is that some may argue that the command to bear children belongs under the "Old Covenant" (or Agreement) in the Bible, which is no longer in effect. It is true that we live under a New Covenant, since Jesus fulfilled the requirements of the old one on our behalf. But we need to remember that there is a part of the Bible that pre-dates that Old Covenant. The command to be fruitful in bearing children is established as part of the *order of creation* in the beginning, and thus remains God's ideal for this planet.

Under the New Covenant, where God's laws are written on our hearts by His Spirit rather than on stone tablets, may we be even more motivated to obey the Lord's every desire as an act of love and devotion. (For a more thorough description of the Old versus New Covenants see the footnote reference at the bottom of the page).[1]

> *"This is the covenant I will make with them*
> *after that time, says the Lord.*
> *I will put my laws in their hearts,*
> *and I will write them on their minds."* (Hebrews 10:16)

---

[1]https://www.thoughtco.com/old-vs-new-covenant-700361

Principle Seven: A Surrendered Womb Does Not Equate Many Children

As you may be growing increasingly nervous as you read, let's establish that *not everyone in the Bible had a large family*. It is clearly not God's will for everyone to have many children, even though we are considered blessed if we do. When we look through the genealogies and stories of the Bible we discover that many families had only two or three children. Some only conceived a few times, even though they lived long enough to have 50 or more children, had God chosen to bless them in that way. Noah, for example, had only three children in his 950-year long life.

Among the large families that we know so well in the Scriptures we discover something significant. King David was Jesse's eighth son, and Joseph was Isaac's eleventh. What if their parents had said, "No Thank You God. Two children, (or even seven) are all we want and can handle." How would history have been different without these men being born to catalyst such breakthroughs for their time? This revelation makes me think of what my own family would look like, had I stopped conceiving after my two oldest children, Ronya and Noa were born. I'm thankful not to have to wonder how the future may look different without my additional children Maya, Mikela, Ezra, Bella, Simba, and Linnea being born "for such a time as this." (Esther 4:14)

"And God said to him, 'I am God Almighty;
be fruitful and increase in number.

A nation and a community of nations

will come from you,

and kings will come from your body.'" (Genesis 35:11)

QUESTIONS

1. Did any Bible text or principle stand out for you in this chapter? If so, list them below.

2. How do you desire to relate to the Scriptures quoted in this chapter? Is there anything you feel the need to study further?

3. What reasons, if any, can you see for Satan trying to thwart God's command to multiply given at creation?

CHAPTER THREE
WHAT HAPPENED TO THE SCRIPTURAL PARADIGM?

The womb and its fruit have been attacked in numerous ways throughout History. The Bible lets us know that the devil prowls around like a "roaring lion looking for someone to devour" (1Peter 5:8). It makes sense that he would target the most helpless and defenseless humans in his pursuit; the unborn. If he can prevent us from being born he won't need to exert himself in keeping us away from our Kingdom purpose during our lives.

In this chapter, we will look at what happened to the view of the womb and fertility through the ages. How did we travel from a time where people desired many children, and allowed the body to function according to its natural hormonal cycle, to where we are today? We will look at societal paradigm shifts, our own choices because of them, and external changes in the world around us. All of these factors contribute to the enemy's success in keeping women's wombs empty during most of their childbearing years.

Paradigm Shifts in the World and in the Church

In our recent history, we see much social change directly resulting from the influence of the Women's Liberation Movement. Simultaneously with the increase of "equality" between the sexes an undermining of God's divine order in the world occurred. As women gained increasing confidence and freedom, (a beautiful thing in and of itself), fertility became a threat. Being financially independent, and pursuing careers over building homes, are now the societal norm. Marriages are falling apart at alarming rates, while gender confusion explodes. Somehow, these facts are like beads strung together on the same string; linked and closely related. Suddenly, the very definition of what family *is*, is up for debate. But families are and will always be the foundation of every nation, just like cells are the building blocks of a body.

In the book "Radical Feminism," Sheila Cronan claims that the women's liberation movement has to abolish the institution of marriage in order to be successful in its mission, since marriage equals "slavery for women"[2]. To give you a further glimpse into the trajectory of the feminists' freedom agenda here are two quotes by well-known feminist leaders; Vivian Gornick and Margaret Sanger:

> *Being a housewife is an illegitimate profession... The choice to serve and be*

---

[2]Sheila Cronan, *Marriage,* in Koedt, Levine and Rapone, *Radical Feminism,* (New York, Times Books, 1973), 219.

protected and plan towards being a family- maker is a choice that shouldn't be.
The heart of radical feminism is to change that.[3]

The most merciful thing a large family can do to one of its infant members is
to kill it.[4]

Whether plainly stated in the media or not, the agenda of the feminist movement is seeping into the very fabric of our world. Growing up, I was never *explicitly* taught that my womb is for me to control, or that bearing children is an inconvenience, or that I have more important things to do than building a healthy family. These thoughts simply became mine by default. As if I inhaled them from unspoken values around me. A closed womb, which in the Bible is a curse, is how I preferred my womb most of the time. And an open womb, which according to God is a blessing, seemed a very scary and unpredictable thing. Back then, it never entered my mind that the womb may still be one of God's chosen pathways to fill the Earth with His presence and glory.

There is not much talk of God's plan for the womb in Christian circles. In general, the teachings in the Scriptures concerning the womb are largely out of view in the church. Perhaps not intentionally, but more like a blind spot. There are a few voices that speak up such as those from the Pro-Life Movement. Lou Engle, a powerful revivalist intercessor and pro-life proponent in America, is one of these voices.

---

[3]Vivian Gornick, *The Daily Illini*, (Illinois, Illini Media Company, April 25, 1981).
[4]Margaret Sanger, *Women and the New Race*, (New York, Brentano's Publishers, 1920), 67.

My husband Trace was 45 years old, and we had three children, when he got ahold of a cassette tape (remember those days) with Mr. Engle's testimony. In it he challenged people to fully give over control of the womb to the Lord. Coming face-to-face with this appeal to surrender my husband had the same revelation I had before our third child was born. Due to Trace's desire to be a wholehearted follower of Jesus, he couldn't keep our family planning from the Lord any more. The excuses and fears of being too old, too poor, too busy etc. had to give way to God's perfect will. At that time my husband and I agreed that we would not only believe in the pro-life message, but *live it* practically by trusting God with the fruitfulness of my womb.

Looking at church history, we find that our modern family planning paradigm is quite a new phenomenon among believers. Until the 19th century all Christians; whether Catholic, Orthodox, Anglican, or Protestant, agreed that contraception is against the order God put in place for humans. It was expected for all believers to leave the control of the womb to God. Today mostly orthodox Catholics still publicly hold this view.

For the Jews, whose Bible is the Old Testament, birth control was equally unthinkable a few generations ago. For further study on this topic I advise visiting the recommended links on the Jewish site Chabad.org.[5] The teachings on the website give insight into the Jewish honor of the

---

[5]https://www.chabad.org/therebbe/letters/default_cdo/aid/2307921/jewish/Part-II-Reproduction-Chapter-V-Birth-Control-and-Contraception.htm

sacredness of the womb, and God's supremacy in the timing of childbirth. I've found that even present-day Jewish authors and teachers encourage Jews to "be fruitful and increase in number,"[6] and receive as many children as God would grant.[7] The Jewish Sacred writings in the Talmud even go as far as comparing refusing to birth life to taking a life.

> *Every man is obligated to marry a woman in order to be fruitful, and to multiply and anyone who doesn't engage in being fruitful and multiplying is as if he spills blood. (Shulchan Arukh, Even HaEzer 1:1)[8]*

The Choice of Aborting and Rejecting Pregnancies

The women in the Bible found such satisfaction and purpose in the *honor* of bearing children. These mothers paint a stark contrast to females today, who mostly desire closed wombs. Furthermore, in recent years, we have taken the reversal of God's order of creation to a completely new level. Although abortion existed in primitive forms for many decades, we have made it an efficient, legal, popular, money-making business. So radically do we desire to control our lives that we readily kill our own offspring to do so. The ability to terminate pregnancies at will now represents an easy path to freedom and relief. As if nothing great was at stake.

---

[6]Genesis 1:28

[7]https://www.chabad.org/library/article_cdo/aid/481962/jewish/What-is-the-Torahs-view-on-birth-control.htm

[8]See also Yevamot 63b:16

"Woe to those who call evil good and good evil,

who put darkness for light and light for darkness,

who put bitter for sweet and sweet for bitter.

Woe to those who are wise in their own eyes

and clever in their own sight." (Isaiah 5:20)

In God's eyes, a baby in the womb carries the same value as any human being. From His perspective, there is no time when a fetus is not yet a "living soul." His plans and love for us extend back even before we enter the womb. If someone injured a pregnant woman in the Old Testament, and she lost her child because of it, the cost was a life for a life (Exodus 21:22-23). In other words, killing a fetus incurred the same punishment as murdering any other person.

An online abortion counter, based on the most current statistics, report that more than 1,500,000,000 abortions have taken place worldwide since 1980. Over 61,000,000 lives have been killed in this fashion in America since 1973, when the pro-choice law "Roe versus Wade" came into effect.[9] These are staggering unfathomable numbers! (For more information on Roe versus Wade see the footnote reference below).[10] Among many other statistics found in their free download the CareNet organization concludes that 21% of all U.S. pregnancies end in abortion[11]. Facts compiled prove that one in four women in America has an abortion in their life time.[12] No

---

[9]http://www.numberofabortions.com/
[10]https://en.wikipedia.org/wiki/Roe_v._Wade
[11]https://resources.care-net.org/free-resources/
[12]https://www.guttmacher.org/report/abortion-incidence-service-availability-us-2017

wonder the prophetic warning of God's cup of wrath filling up is echoing over the land, as the blood of all these innocent ones "cry out from the ground"[13].

Life Way research reports that 70% of women who had abortions in 2015 professed Christianity as their faith of choice. 43% attended church regularly.[14] (If you are one of these women who had an abortion, please read Diana's story in Appendix II. There is an abundance of grace and restoration for us in Jesus!) But even for those of us who consider abortion an unthinkable option, we often make choices that *prevent* pregnancies, for the same reasons as others terminate them. During most of our childbearing years, we make the choice to prevent pregnancies based on inconvenience, expense, untimeliness, discomfort, risk etc.

External Factors Affecting Fertility

The detrimental effect of sin on this planet over time is now doing its own part in keeping wombs closed and barren. The air we breathe, the chemically laden and processed food we eat, the beauty products we apply, the cleaners and detergents we use, the plastic containers and cooking utensils we need, even the water we drink, contain harmful pollutants. These chemicals alter the hormonal balance in our systems and cause increasing infertility. Even when conception happens, the body finds it

---

[13]In Gen. 4:10 the idea is presented that the life-blood of a person wrongfully killed cries out for justice when "spilled on the ground."
[14]https://lifewayresearch.com/2015/11/23/women-distrust-church-on-abortion/

harder to sustain pregnancies due to the numerous unchecked toxins in our bodies.

> *It is believed that environmental contaminants may cause infertility by creating other health conditions. For example, some research suggests that environmental contaminants can affect a woman's menstruation and ovulation. Low-level exposures to compounds such as phthalates, polychlorinated biphenyls (PCBs), dioxin, and pesticides are suspected risk factors.* [15]

Another alarming reason why many wombs don't function well today is the various contraceptives that disturb natural hormonal balance in a woman's body. Having used these pregnancy preventions for some time it is a big adjustment for the body to get back to normal and actually conceive. Once we feel the timing is right for us to have a baby, the body may feel otherwise. Professionals specializing in women's health frequently discover that women may not ovulate for up to three years after taking the pill. This hibernating hormonal state is the result of the contraceptives suppressing the reproductive system for too long.[16]

It appears we cannot take fertility for granted, as something to turn off and on at will. The enemy, using whatever means he can, has an agenda against the womb. I don't intend to bring discouragement to those desiring to have children, but rather to sound an alarm. The womb is a most sacred gift that is under attack. May we understand the battle we are in and cover

---

[15]http://ephtracking.cdc.gov/showRbFertilityInfertilityEnv.action
[16]Marilyn Glenville, *Natural Solutions to Infertility*, (London, Piatkus Books, 2000).

our family-destinies in prayer. Because we desperately need God's protection of the womb as we desire to conceive, we find even more reason to allow Jesus the Lordship over our fertility. Let's be encouraged by this simple yet powerful quote by the first mother, Eve, which emphasize God's partnership with us in birthing life:

"With the help of the Lord I have brought forth a man."
(Genesis 4:1)

QUESTIONS

1. Have you ever heard a sermon or Bible study on God's purpose for the womb, or read a Christian book on family planning? What message did it contain and how did it impact you?

2. What have you known about the agenda of the feminist movement?

3. Do you know anyone who terminated a pregnancy, or have you? What is their/your story post abortion?

CHAPTER FOUR
A GENERATION NEEDING TO BE BORN

The fruit of the womb carries the greatest potential gifts for humankind; gifts that can change the course of history forever. In this chapter, we will look at how we desperately need wombs to open for God's champions to be conceived in our time.

In the Bible, we read that Sarah had a closed womb. This is the first account of a woman not able to conceive since creation. Surely it was not a coincidence that Sarah's womb experienced this abnormal state of fruitlessness. She was called to be the mother of God's chosen people and I'm sure there was a cosmic battle over her destiny. The same was true of Rachel, another mother in the Old Testament, who for a season also had a closed womb. As God eventually lifted her disgrace and filled her womb, she became the mother of Joseph who saved God's people from starvation during a devastating famine. The list continues with Hannah, who was barren, but had the call to be the mother of a powerful line of prophets. Elisabeth, the mother of John the Baptist, who prepared the way for Jesus Himself, was also barren until her old age when she finally bore her son.

When I was pregnant with my sixth child, a woman who I barely knew came up to my big belly with a word from God. She told me that the child I was carrying was very important. She said that it was as if God had been asking, "Who will I give this one to? Who will receive her without questioning Me?" At this moment, I don't know what Bella's divine purpose is in the earth, but what I do know is that if I had said "No thank You," God may have had to give her to someone else. But what happens when there are not enough people who accept the children needing to be born at a certain time and place in history? What happens when most people say, "No thank You," or "Not now," to God's plan for the expansion of families on the earth?

The core message of this book is that there are children that need to be born for God's purpose to be fulfilled in the generations and nations of the earth. This chapter is where we dive into the real implications of the statement God spoke to me, with which I started this book:

> *You think in terms of me, mine, and the here and now.*
> *I think in terms of generations and nations.*

Recently, I had a vision where I saw the air thick with seeds. They were the kind of seeds we blow off dandelions to make a wish. As they simply hung in mass in the sky above me, every now and then one would drop down to the ground. But millions only hovered, waiting for their turn. I knew each seed represented a child waiting to be born on the earth. It is beyond me to fathom the repercussions of wombs not opening to receive the seeds God wishes to plant on earth.

Of one thing I am certain; His plans to transform generations and nations must be linked to our "Yes" or "No" in giving birth to His chosen. We pray for God's work in the earth to be finished, and we long for Jesus' return. Yet we hesitate to give life to the children who will accomplish the task and prepare the way for the Eternal Kingdom, even after we are gone.

Individualistic or Nationalistic Thinking

In the Western church at large we embrace a very short-sighted view of life and the world, and one that is hugely individualistic. Many times, we don't think further than our own personal life, or the life of our immediate family. But the Kingdom of God is dependent on each of its members functioning in their God given roles. A Kingdom can never be stronger than its individual units. Whatever decisions we make in our homes undoubtedly affect the Body of Christ as a whole, and thus the Kingdom of God in the Earth. It is all connected.

The Jews naturally seem to have a clearer understanding of, and solidarity to, their nationhood than Christians. The Jewish Rabbi, Menachem Mendel Schneerson, is one of the religious authorities who emphasize that the Torah does not support free use of birth control. In the "Igrot Kodesh" (Holy Epistles) he teaches that the number of children God wants to bestow upon a family is not merely a private concern, since the Jew is part of a larger people group. The decisions of the individual naturally affect the nation as a whole.[17] And to shock you a bit, here is a quote by a Muslim:

---

[17]Igros Kodesh, Vol. IV, p. 76

A national policy of family planning which aims to reduce the population is unacceptable because it is likely to have serious repercussion on the health of the nation as a whole.[18]

Abraham's two sons, Isaac and Ishmael, were both destined to become great nations. Even today, both the Jews (the sons of Isaac) and the Muslims (the Arabs from the line of Ishmael) maintain a sense of national loyalty and pride. They understand that the decisions each family makes impact their people group, with which they feel connection and solidarity. As Christians, however, we seem to lack understanding of the truth that we are also a *nation*.

The Kingdom of God that we belong to has unseen borders. Our signifying mark and family trait is not a particular look or national flag, as is the case for Jews or Muslims. Ours is the "invisible" seal of God's Spirit, which in no way diminishes the fact that we are a nation. We are here on this planet, scattered as ambassadors among all the different countries of the world. But, according to the Bible, our citizenship is in heaven (Philippians 3:20).

> **"But you are a chosen people, a royal priesthood,**
> **a holy nation, a people belonging to God,**
> **that you may declare the praises of him**
> **who called you out of darkness**
> **into his wonderful light." (1 Peter 2:9)**

---

[18]https://www.missionislam.com/family/familyplanning.htm

In fact, our impact and influence in the world has the potential to be even more invasive and widespread because of our fluidity as a nation without borders. According to Jesus, our effect on this world as we spread the culture of His Kingdom, is as invasive as yeast that permeates the dough (Matthew 13:33). This influence is also likened to salt that flavors everything for the better, and light that makes the darkness flee (Matthew 5:13-14).

"The wind blows wherever it pleases.
You hear its sound,
but you cannot tell where it comes from
or where it is going.
So it is with everyone born of the Spirit." (John 3:8)

Numbers Do Matter

The Bible explains that when we become believers in Jesus, we are grafted into the family tree of Abraham and his descendants, the Jews. As we merge with them as a people, we receive the same inheritance and blessing that God gave the Israelites long ago. Part of the promised blessing includes having an offspring that is more *numerous* than the stars in the sky (Genesis 15:5). The reason for growing numerous, apart from the simple fact that God loves His children, is to have an increased impact in the world. As heirs with Abraham we equally inherit the role of showing the rest of the world who God is. This is not a small task and not one without opposition. It is also a task that is more efficiently accomplished with large amounts of people.

> *"The LORD made his people very fruitful;*
> *he made them too numerous for their foes."* **(Psalm 105:24)**

The devil always delights in working against the promises and prophecies that predict God's people positively impacting the world. The Holocaust, where it's estimated that 6 million Jews were killed,[19] is such a stark example of this bent on destruction. The reason for this massacre was the same as the first big massacre we know about from Scripture. What Hitler and the Egyptian Pharaoh in the book of Exodus have in common, is the fear of God's people becoming *too numerous* and thus too influential. These evil men knew what we as Christians must also understand; numbers do matter!

> *"Then a new king, who did not know about Joseph,*
> *came to power in Egypt.*
> *'Look,' he said to his people,*
> *'the Israelites have become much too numerous for us.'*
> *. . . Then Pharaoh gave this order to all his people:*
> *'Every boy that is born you must throw into the Nile.'"*
> **(Exodus 1:8,9,22)**

---

[19]https://encyclopedia.ushmm.org/content/en/article/documenting-numbers-of-victims-of-the-holocaust-and-nazi-persecution

In the nations where Christianity is rapidly growing numerically, there is also proof of opposition and persecution. The fact that we see very little persecution of believers in the west is probably a sign that we don't significantly challenge status quo in society or the kingdom of darkness. We do not increase fast enough, by births or conversions, to pose any real threat to anything. But this will change!

I am a firm believer in the many prophetic promises of the large harvest of souls coming into God's Kingdom. And I also believe that we are meant to birth those who will help bring in this harvest. The fact that we need to open our wombs to these chosen ones does not take away the honor that should be given to people who adopt sons and daughters. Adoption is a wonderful way of gaining souls for eternity and fulfilling God's heart to place the lonely in families and care for the orphans.[20] But obedience to one command does not cancel out obedience to another. I believe that God calls us to surrender in such a way that we are willing to take in *whomever* God sends for us to care for in our families. They may come by birth, adoption, conversion, or all three.

A Time of Favor for Increase

Because darkness is increasing in the earth and the Kingdom of Light needs manpower, I feel an urgency as I'm writing the message in this book.

---

[20]Psalm 68:6, Psalm 82:3

There is a window of time that is getting shorter, in which a crucial generation needs to be born.

Jesus prophesied that times are coming when it will be difficult to be pregnant or nursing (Matthew 24:19). I believe that a time with legalized restrictions and consequences to childbearing could eventually come to the western part of the world. Currently population control is a hot topic of discussion in many modern nations.[21] But it's not a new subject. "Eugenics" (the practice of restricting certain genetic traits of "weaker" population groups by preventing reproduction by law/force) was practiced in Europe, the United Sates and Canada in the early 20th century.[22] Historically and currently the US also applies various population stunting practices to their foreign policies in third world countries, as the famous "Kissinger Report" outlines.[23] Thankfully there is an uprising to protect life and freedom in America today, supported by much prayer but this agenda is not without its own vicious enemies. I believe that now is a time of favor and preparation for believing families. It is my prayer that we use this time of grace to reach new levels of abandon, and let God use our homes to raise His "crazy" Jesus lovers. Lets equally trust that He will close our wombs when our time to birth children is over.

These days there are many books published and sermons preached about the Biblical prophecy of "turning the hearts of the fathers to the children"

---

[21]http://www.scientificamerican.com/article/population-and-sustainablilty/
[22]http://en.m.wikipedia.org/wiki/Eugenics
[23]http://pdf.usaid.gov/pdf_docs/Pcaab500.pdf

(Malachi 4:6). The call is going out for mature believers to awaken and prepare to father and mother the incoming harvest of souls. In this book, we talk about one of the ways that hearts of fathers and mothers have hardened and turned away from sons and daughters; namely in *not allowing them to be born.*

I believe that the perspective of birthing and parenting our own offspring adds another piece to the fulfillment of the Malachi prophecy. It is time we welcome the children, by allowing them entry into our families, for a much larger purpose than we may have seen. I am convinced that there are souls with destinies equivalent to that of Elijah, David, Joseph, Esther, and Daniel in the Scriptures, just waiting to be born in this age. Their calling is the highest imaginable; to make the way straight for the coming of the King, and the restoration of all things.

> *"In the wilderness prepare the way for the Lord;*
> *make straight in the desert a highway for our God.*
> *Every valley shall be raised up,*
> *every mountain and hill made low;*
> *the rough ground shall become level,*
> *the rugged places plain.*
> *And the glory of the Lord will be revealed,*
> *and all people will see it together."* **(Isaiah 40:3-5)**

A Generation Like None Other

If our young people knew the powerful and thrilling nation and generation in which they have an irreplaceable role, they would grow up with a sense of purpose that would make them unstoppable. Is it any wonder we lose so many of them to other forms of "belonging" when we don't have a strong sense of nationhood or family in the Body of Christ? We are created to belong. We crave to know our identity. Watch and wonder as this generation discover who they really are!

> *"You have made them to be a kingdom*
> *and priests to serve our God,*
> *and they will reign on the earth."* (Revelation 5:10)

The last generation of Christian believers will probably look like nothing we have ever seen. Many may be offended at this "new wine skin generation." Its wine may not appeal to many a religious palate (Luke 5:38-39). But God is not worried about that. He is not afraid to offend. He has generations and nations to win for eternity.

> *"I tell you the truth, anyone who has faith in me*
> *will do what I have been doing.*
> *He will do even greater things than these."* (John 14:12)

We learn from the Scriptures that creation itself yearns for these special Sons of God to arise (Romans 8:19). The Bible explains that this group is such a force to be reckoned with that heaven and earth tremble as they approach (Joel 2). I pray that the vision of this powerful army of lovers, who overcome evil with good and darkness with light; who walk with authority in all spheres of life, and who prepare the way for the King of Glory, comes alive in our minds.

May we no longer think primarily about "me, mine, and the here and now," but rather lay down our lives for generations to come and for the salvation of nations. As citizens of the Nation and Kingdom of God, may we understand that the decisions we make in our family units affect a much grander purpose. If we entrust our family planning to God, more children will surely be born. Not to all of us, but probably to many. And as these children grow, many more workers will be sent out to the harvest for the expansion of the Kingdom of Light. Those whom God intends to be will indeed become, and who knows what that may mean for humanity!

QUESTIONS

1. Growing up, did you feel a sense of belonging and identity in the Body of Christ? Did you think of yourself as someone destined for greatness?

2. How does being challenged to see yourself as a part of a "nation of believers," and a Kingdom that is not of this world, make you feel?

3. How do you feel about the idea that your individual family decisions affect the "nation of believers" and God's kingdom as a whole?

CHAPTER FIVE
EXAMINING MIND-SETS THAT OPPOSE
THE WOMB

Despite the many external weapons the enemy uses to keep wombs empty, his most successful battlefield against the unborn is undoubtedly our minds. So many of his victories happen in *paradigms* and *mindsets*. In the next two chapters I will share some thoughts in response to the most common arguments for not surrendering our wombs to God. Note that whole books could be written on each of these topics. We only take a brief look at each one, for the sake of provoking thought.

In this chapter, we bring up two objections that deal with wider philosophical ways of seeing the world and the future.

Reasoning One: "It is selfish to have many children at a time when the world is becoming overpopulated"

Every year, new statistics come out regarding the issue of overpopulation on planet Earth. The statistics make claims that in a certain amount of years, if the birth-rate and death-rate are such and such, the resources of the planet will cover only so much of the need. The debate on overpopulation has become a household topic of discussion. The media made sure of it. As in many cases the stirring up of *fear*, (in this case fear of lack), is used to motivate people to be ready for some kind of change (problem-reaction-solution).

The question is, what kind of change can we anticipate as a solution to a topic as this, and at what cost? Well, something must change, mustn't it? If birth rates stay the same we may not have enough food and resources for everyone, right? Already in 1963, the National Academy of Sciences concluded that *"Either the birth rate of the world must come down or the death rate must go back up."*[24]

It turns out that this way of interpreting the statistics on the earth's population is only one way of looking at things. If we search a little deeper, we find studies claiming we have plenty of resources for everyone on the planet. The uneven distribution of the existing wealth on earth is really the problem. As well as the apparent unwillingness of society at large to look for a solution as to how to provide for everyone. The effort and large amounts of finances (tax money) are seemingly rather used in many creative ways to decrease the earth's population. All the while making sure the standard of living is maintained for the top consumers on the planet (justified survival of the fittest).

To further confuse the matter, we now hear voices say the exact opposite of population control advocates. Even back in 2004, Newsweek magazine

---

[24]National Academy of Sciences, *The Growth of World Population: Analysis of the Problems and Recommendations for Research and Training*, (Washington, DC, The National Academies Press, 1963).

stated: *"Remember the population bomb? The new threat to the planet is not too many people, but too few."[25]* At present, an increasing amount of statistics predict the consequences of this "new threat" to the indigenous population of many industrialized countries, due to our choices *not* to have children. The cogwheels of society are becoming seriously disturbed, as there is not enough of a workforce growing up to support the large number of retirees.[26]

The machinery of western countries is still ticking on though, partially with the help of the immigrant population. It is not my intention to discuss the implications this trend has on the fabric of societies and cultures, but to leave that to your own discernment. I do encourage awareness concerning the fact that the family paradigms and religious convictions of the Muslim immigrants encourage having many children. Due to this fact alone, both their culture and religion become an increasing influence in the west over time. While the populations in Europe and America are shrinking, the UN predicts that the Middle East will double its population by 2031.[27]

The "mother of birth-control," Margaret Sanger, had a very painful past which motivated her extensive work in educating women on preventing births. Her mother was a devote Catholic who had 18 children in 20 years, and died in her 50's. On top of her mother's untimely death, Margaret

---

[25]Michael Meyer, *Birth Dearth,* Newsweek International, September 27, 2004, (New York, Newsweek International, 2004).

[26]https://foreignpolicy.com/2017/07/03/heres-who-will-lament-and-celebrate-the-plummeting-u-s-birth-rate-babies-abortion-immigration-europe/

[27]http://www.life.org.nz/abortion/abortionkeyissues/impactonsociety2

witnessed many self-induced and detrimental abortions in her lifetime, which left women suffering.

Out of Margaret's negative paradigm concerning childbearing, stemmed from resentment and pain, grew a movement fueled by powerful forces. It eventually formed a global abortion and population-control machine.[28] The work of this organization, that we now know as the Planned Parenthood Federation of America, couples the values of Margaret Sanger with tax payers' money. Taking advantage of scared, insecure, and easily influenced mothers-to-be, they move their twisted agenda along.

> *Planned Parenthood claims abortion is inseparable from their mission, and with half of their budget coming from taxpayers, it's safe to say our tax dollars are inseparable from their abortion mission. Recent annual reports show Planned Parenthood's dramatic increase in taxpayer funding has led them to expand abortion while cutting clients and other health services.[29]*

The opposition of Planned Parenthood claims that the sole purpose of the movement is to control, manipulate, and decrease the Earth's population, all in the name of caring for women's rights. This claim is now supported by unveilings in the media, one of which is the release of the previously classified "Jaffe Memo". This memorandum, written in 1969, contains a long list of proposed strategies on reducing the population, composed by the vice president of Planned Parenthood at the time.

---

[28]http://en.wikipedia.org/wiki/Margaret_Sanger
[29]https://rtl.org/RLMNews/09editions/AreMyTaxDollarsPayingForAbortion.htm

The Jaffe Memo suggestions range from altering social ideals regarding marriage, womanhood and family, and encouraging homosexual relations; to proposals of putting fertility suppressants in public water, and invoking compulsory abortion and sterilization.[30] Many of the strategies in this memorandum have been applied and as a result have detrimentally affected our society long term.

When women were crying along the path as Jesus carried the cross up to Golgotha, He told them not to weep for Him, but rather for the days coming when people would call a barren womb and dry breast "good". In contrast to the agenda of governments today that encourage empty wombs, Jesus says for us to mourn such a reality. This naturally implies that full wombs and nursing breasts are a natural cause for celebration in Jesus' eyes.

"Jesus turned and said to them,
'Daughters of Jerusalem, do not weep for me;
weep for yourselves and for your children.
For the time will come when you will say,
'Blessed are the barren women,
the wombs that never bore
and the breasts that never nursed!'" **(Luke 23:28-29)**

[30]https://www.liveaction.org/news/understanding-the-jaffe-memo-planned-parenthoods-disturbing-proposition-of-population-control/

This prophecy by Jesus saw its first fulfillment as the persecution of Christians in Jerusalem happened not long after his death, and pregnant or nursing mothers immediately suffered. Times like that have come and gone throughout history in different nations since. But I don't believe it is far-fetched to expect specific persecution of those who celebrate pregnancy and nursing in the future. As Planned Parenthood proceeds with their world-wide agenda of preventing births and undermining the role of motherhood, seemingly at any price, things will likely become more absurd than they already are.

The state of New York recently passed a law that allows abortion/murder of a baby at any time during pregnancy, as long as the child is still inside the womb[31]. This law gives us a taste of the demonic forces at work, robbing people of the most foundational instinct of humans; to protect their own young. We don't know what laws and restrictions will be put in place to further achieve desired population control. What we do know is that God knows times and seasons, and sends his messengers to alert us beforehand.

Now is the time for courageous voices to be heard, calling wombs to open, before another "Pharaoh" starts regulating births with more extreme measures out of fear of losing control. May messages calling for absolute surrender; including the surrender of our family planning, permeate the Body of Christ to prepare us for the times ahead.

---

[31]https://www.cbsnews.com/news/new-york-passes-abortion-bill-late-term-if-mothers-health-is-at-risk-today-2019-01-23/

> *"Surely the Sovereign LORD does nothing without revealing his plan to his servants the prophets."*
> **(Amos 3:7)**

The attention given to the discussion on overpopulation in the media is based on the same foundation as all topics in our society; namely one completely depending on human reasoning. As believers however, our starting point for looking at any issue, is the presupposition that God is sovereign, and that "the foolishness of God is wiser than man's wisdom" (1 Corinthians 1:25).

Today, we can find research and information to support almost any view we want proved. Now, more than ever, we need the Holy Spirit's gift of *discernment* (1Corinthians 12:10). This supernatural gift helps us recognize what God's agenda is in every matter and weeds out deception. Satan would love for us to live in fear, based on lies, rather than in surrendered obedience to God's Word.

> *"Dear friends, do not believe every spirit, but test the spirits to see whether they are from God, because many false prophets have gone out into the world."* **(1 John 4:1)**

When it boils down to it, the supposed threat of the world's growing population is an issue that could never be blamed on children being born. The solution to our greed, hording, and over-consumption that depletes and pollutes the earth cannot be abortion or preventing births. Surely the problem of poverty must be solved by fair distribution and living within our means.

If anyone argues that there are too many people born on the planet, maybe we should focus on the rampant sexual activity outside the context of marriage, instead of on the babies themselves. Then, the solution would not be to have fewer children, but to live in abstinence until marriage. Let's allow the Spirit of God to show us the *root causes* of issues around us, so that we don't join the wrong side of the battle and merely fight symptoms. The solution to one sin must not be to commit another one by blaming the innocent unborn.

Let me make the outrageous proposal that *more* people are exactly what this world needs; children born in families committed to furthering God's Kingdom of Light. Imagine if our basic mindset was that humans created in the image of God have the potential for incredible positive change and creative solutions. Then the birth of righteous seed would be the exact thing to desire for these times. The Earth itself is longing for the Sons of God to arise. With divine life, light, love, and creativity they will help bring Heaven to earth as the scripture below suggests. Let's join in this divine desire by partnering with God for the expansion of godly families.

"I consider that our present sufferings
are not worth comparing with the glory
that will be revealed in us.

For the creation waits in eager expectation
for the children of God to be revealed.
For the creation was subjected to frustration,
not by its own choice, but by the will of the one
who subjected it, in hope that the creation itself
will be liberated from its bondage to decay
and brought into the freedom and glory
of the children of God." (Romans 8:18-21)

Reasoning Two: "It is selfish to bring more children into this cruel world, for the sake of the children themselves"

There was a time in my teens when I believed that the above statement was true. For this reason, I didn't think I would have children. In hindsight, I realize how intertwined this thinking was with my limited eschatological understanding (meaning my belief about the future and end of the world). I believed that things were going to get progressively worse on the planet, and that believers who would endure till the end would do so only with great difficulty. I could only foresee suffering increasing so severely, that we would crawl out of the "time of tribulation" exhausted and weary.

Since then, I have encountered an eschatological belief that incorporates the incredible might of God in and through His people. I now see that suffering and tribulation is only one part of the equation. I believe it is thoroughly Scriptural to believe that God's people will be strong, fearless and victorious in those times. Good will overcome the evil trying to take over the world! The light will shine brighter the more darkness prevails.

> *"...so that you may become blameless and pure,*
> *children of God without fault*
> *in a crooked and depraved generation,*
> *in which you shine like stars in the universe."* **(Philippians 2:15)**

> *"And I saw what looked like a sea of glass*
> *mixed with fire and, standing beside the sea,*
> *those who had been victorious*
> *over the beast and his image*
> *and over the number of his name."* **(Revelation 15:2)**

> *"I have given you authority*
> *to trample on snakes and scorpions*
> *and to overcome all the power of the enemy;*
> *nothing will harm you."* **(Luke 10:19)**

There is nothing to fear! God remains faithful to us. He is our strong tower, our provider, our refuge, our strength, and defender. Surely He will also remain so until the end. He has placed His Spirit in us to seal us for eternity. Surely that same Spirit will work in and though us with resurrection power when we need Him the most.

The area where God's people lived during their 400 years of slavery in Egypt was called "Goshen". As God's judgment was poured out on the Egyptians, this area was exempt from the plagues and curses. Even the "angel of death" passed over the homes in Goshen, due to the blood of a lamb painted on their door posts. Jesus encourages us to pray that we will be able to escape the suffering of the last days in like manner (Luke 21:36). We have the covering of the blood of *the* Lamb over our lives!

> **"The days of the blameless are known to the LORD,**
> **and their inheritance will endure forever.**
> *In times of disaster they will not wither;*
> *in days of famine they will enjoy plenty."*
> **(Psalm 37:18-19)**

> *"'On the day when I act,' says the LORD Almighty, 'they will be*
> *my treasured possession.*
> *I will spare them, just as a father has compassion*
> *and spares his son who serves him.*
> *And you will again see the distinction*
> *between the righteous and the wicked,*
> *between those who serve God and those who do not.'"*
> **(Malachi 3:16-18)**

I am sure that many will have a "Goshen-experience" in the last days. Or perhaps an experience like Daniel's, as he sovereignly survived being thrown into a lion's den. Or like Hananiah, Mishael, and Azariah who, when thrown into a blazing furnace, were not singed by the fire. For those who aren't preserved from death, there is no reason to fear. Perhaps they will have a Stephen-like experience. As you may recall from the book of Acts, amid being martyred, all Stephen could see was the glory of God. Being spared suffering or not, God's power and sufficiency will be displayed in and through His people.

Saying that bringing children into this world is cruel implies that their lives will be filled with misery, hardship, and pain. Wouldn't it be more like God to birth children into a cruel world to display His protection, sufficiency, and power? Wouldn't it make more sense for us to expect our "arrows" to be victorious; walking in supernatural power and freedom, defeating evil, and expanding the Kingdom of God wherever they go?

Bearing children for me is not about satisfying my own selfish desires, as some suggest. It is an act of love and obedience to the Lord. (Nonetheless, it is an act of obedience that brings me great joy and pleasure!) In fact, when surrendered believers give birth, I believe it's a service to both God and mankind. I don't prophesy doom over my children by expecting their future to be dreadful. I share with them what the word of God teaches:

"You, dear children, are from God
and have overcome them,
because the one who is in you is greater
than the one who is in the world." (1 John 4:4)

"In all these things we are more than conquerors through him who loved us." **(Romans 8:37)**

On a more personal note, I confess that I once believed that since we raise our children to be overcomers, they would be spared from much temptation and struggle. As I watched one of my beautiful arrows with oxygen tubes, gadgets, and drips attached to the body, waking up from a drug and alcohol induced coma, this idealism vanished. I have since repented of pridefully believing I possessed the ability to raise mighty men and women of God.

It is by God's Spirit as Helper, and through Him *only,* that we can parent a generation under such onslaught from the enemy. The ferociousness with which the demonic attacks these young ones, and the cunningness with which it deceives and distracts them, should enrage us. When it does, may we cry out to the only One who can and *will* help them overcome.

We must not stand in judgment of the struggles our children face. We don't have to walk their walk during this dark time of history. Neither can we lose sight of their true identity, even as we wait for them to see and believe it themselves. Every now and then I get a divine glimpse into the glory and treasure that the youth of today carry for this time in history. It overwhelms me with marvel and awe!

Many times I have looked into the eyes of my older ones during struggles and failures, and told them that I *know* who they are, despite of what they are going through. This always makes flickers of hope appear in their countenance, as truth pierces the deception that tries to confuse and discourage them from their calling.

As I see my children conquering today, and growing in their identity as kings and queens in the Kingdom of God, I am less afraid of the fact that they will overcome very real and dangerous obstacles along the way. I am convinced that they will walk in holiness and the power of the Most High God! After all, He is the one who gave them to our family for such a time as this, and He is well able to keep His own. The credit for their victories goes to God. The glory of their conquests belongs to Him alone. I am so grateful for God's grace as a mother in this generation. Now more than ever.

QUESTIONS

1. What is your thinking concerning the debate on overpopulation? Does your way of viewing the world make you feel worried or fearful?

2. What is your understanding of the state of God's people at the end of the world? Is this a view based on fear?

3. After reading this chapter do you find anything in your paradigm worth questioning and seeking God on further?

CHAPTER SIX
EXAMINING FEARS CONCERNING THE OPEN WOMB

In this chapter we discuss the personal fears that dominate many minds when considering having multiple children. These fears are largely based on lies the enemy wants us to embrace. Let's read this chapter with open minds, and allow God's Spirit to prepare a way in our hearts for our best adventure yet. And remember, surrendering your womb to God doesn't automatically mean you receive a dozen children. It's an openness to His perfect plan that we are after, no matter the ultimate number.

Reasoning One: "I can't have more than two or three children. It is just too hard!"

This is a very common remark people make as they see our big family of ten. I always gladly admit that there are days when I feel absolutely overwhelmed . . . just as I did when I had only one child. Child rearing in general isn't an easy occupation. The truth is, I feel less overwhelmed now than I did when I first became a mother. I'm convinced that the hardest transition we face is from being a childless couple to caring for someone else around the clock.

The idea people generally have is that because it is challenging to have one child, and sometimes harder to have two, it must get progressively more difficult with each one. This is simply *not* true! I didn't become a mother of eight overnight. I gradually grew into it. By the time child number three came along, living with multiple children had become a habit. Also, consider this; children who grow up in big families normally become helpers at a quicker rate than in smaller families, which fosters maturity and responsibility. As new little ones are born, there are multiple helping hands available for different tasks in the home. Jennifer Flanders, an active blogger on family issues and mother of twelve, says it like this:

> *A wise man once observed, "Many hands make light labor." He was right. Of course, many hands make bigger messes to begin with, but when everyone pitches in to help clean up, household chores are knocked out in short order, and kids learn responsibility and other important life skills from an early age.*[32]

Already at age two, toddlers are old enough to obey simple commands that make a mother's life easier. The beautiful thing is that at this age they normally love to help. As they learn that this is expected early on it becomes part of how they operate. (Admitted this takes more work with some than others, but it is time well spent!) We may also find that as a new member of the family arrives, with all the joy it brings, even those who may be reluctant to help suddenly want to be mini-mom or dad. It's so

---

[32]https://lovinglifeathome.com/2014/02/13/15-unexpected-benefits-of-big-family-living/

beautiful to see what a new life brings out in older siblings. Even the toughest of teens melts while cuddling a baby.

About seven years ago, I discovered that I had hit a completely new stage of freedom in my role as a mother. My oldest daughter had turned twelve and become the best babysitter we had ever known. My five- and six-year-olds were becoming more familiar with their homeschooling requirements, and my ten-year-old son started acting as self-motivated as my oldest daughter in getting his work done (knowing he could play once he finished). Suddenly I realized that at times I could leave home to run errands, or have coffee with a friend, all by myself. I didn't need to wait until the youngest had turned twelve, only until one was mature enough to safely hold down the fort.

At the time of writing this chapter, my youngest child is two and a half years old and we just found out that I'm pregnant! Due to our house being full of expert baby-sitters and helpers, I am able to pursue some passions that have been dormant for years. Also, since we made a faith leap and moved to America to enroll the children in an amazing Christian school four days a week, I only have two little ones at home most days.

I'm learning to embrace seasons of a messier house and a more hectic schedule, as well as phases of inactivity and mostly being home with diapers and dishes. God's timing is perfect, and seasons constantly change. Our family can't wait for another little one to arrive! Personally, I am ready for the down time of nursing and enjoying this precious life.

I know people with one child, who are constantly stressed, and never feel like they have time for anything but changing diapers and feeding. I also know big families who, by helping each other, can live with both peace and fulfillment. These large families are somehow still able to travel, enjoy cultural experiences, have a social life and pursue their passions and callings. I have a vision of the latter for our family. I find that having that mindset opens many doors for us to see the world, share life with incredible people, grow in and express our creative gifts etc.

The need for help should not be belittled in the scenario of big family life though. At times, someone has cleaned my house once a week, or just deep cleaned the kitchen. At another time, we had a mother's helper stay with us a few weeks at the time of a birth. Other friends of ours have live-in helpers, either for taking care of the home, helping with the children, or both. Different seasons may call for different reinforcements, and different families have need or means for more help than others.

It is not a lie that it is hard to have many children, but it is definitely a lie that it is *too* hard. It is not too hard *if* it is God's plan for us. If God asks us to do something, He always gives us all the provision, grace, and strength to carry it out. The inclination to run away from things that are hard is a product of the instant-gratification-mentality that permeates present day society. "Hard" however, is often what leads to awesome things.

"Not only so, but we also rejoice in our sufferings,

because we know that suffering produces perseverance;

perseverance, character; and character, hope."

(Romans 5:3-4)

"For whoever wants to save their life will lose it,

but whoever loses their life for me will find it."

(Matthew 16:25)

I believe that just as God intends for us to help our children mature, they are meant to do the same for us. In fact, the parallel growth that happens as we parent and learn to manage our families well, is the very thing that qualifies us to minister to God's people according to the apostle Paul (1 Timothy 3:2-5). There is no time we face ourselves more honestly and fully, as when facing our own children. There certainly arise ugly sides of us that we had no idea existed. It is very humbling to live with the constant reminder that we are not as perfect as we once believed.

Parenting may be a challenging job, but if more of us were taught about the beauty of servanthood, and the rewards that come with it, we may be more open to it. Becoming a parent means there is room for less of "me," but what if that's not a bad thing? In fact, the very best thing we can do, according to God, is to lay down our life for the sake of someone else (John 15:13).

"Each of you should look not only to your own interests, but also to the interests of others.

Your attitude should be the same as that of Christ Jesus:
Who, being in very nature God,
did not consider equality with God
something to be grasped, but made himself nothing,
taking the very nature of a servant,
being made in human likeness. **(Philippians 2:4-7)**

Perhaps God wants you to have only one or two children. Perhaps He wants you to have more. The point is that with each one comes the added grace for the task.

Reasoning Two: "Having more children is too expensive"

I have heard it said that the most difficult thing for us to trust God with is our wallet. I would like to say that it is equally hard, if not harder, for us to trust Him with our family planning. But a valid point it is. I cannot tell you how many times I hear believers, myself included, utter the words, *"I can't do that. It's too expensive".* Although I still catch myself thinking like that, I try to replace this reasoning with a question: *"Does God want me to do it?"* If I become convinced that the answer is *yes*, then I must move forward trusting provision will come, at the right time.

While discussing walking by faith in the area of finances, a dear friend of mine who is a new believer said, "Money doesn't rain down from heaven, does it?!" Well, although it definitely could (Jesus paid his taxes from coins found in the mouth of a fish), it normally doesn't. Either way, let's not get stuck in thinking about provision merely in the ways of the world. God often provides in ways I cannot foresee or figure out myself, which requires trust. A woman of God who enjoys many supernatural encounters with Jesus named Kat Kerr, explains: *"In the Kingdom of God we don't make a living to exist. We exist to LIVE."* In fact, basing our life-decisions on money is an absolute no-go in Jesus' teachings, as these scriptures express:

"No one can serve two masters.
Either you will hate the one and love the other,
or you will be devoted to the one
and despise the other.
You cannot serve both God and money." **(Matthew 6:24)**

"So do not worry, saying, 'What shall we eat?'
or 'What shall we drink?'
or 'What shall we wear?'
For the pagans run after all these things,
and your heavenly Father knows
that you need them." **(Matthew 6:31-32)**

Once, as our financial situation looked particularly bleak from an earthly perspective, I had a dream. In the dream there was a map pointing for our family to go to Vienna, which means "forest stream." In the dream I knew this location represented *peace* (Psalm 23). The next location on the map was a place called *Provision*, but there was no visible road there. All I knew was that once we reached Vienna (peace), the next leg of the journey would show itself. The important lesson in the dream impacted me greatly. Unless we reach peace by trusting in the Lord, *before* provision shows up, our peace is based on the provision itself, rather than the Provider.

"The lions may grow weak and hungry,
but those who seek the LORD lack no good thing." (Psalm 34:10)

"I was young and now I am old, yet I have never seen the righteous forsaken or their children begging bread." (Psalm 37:25)

One of the most important lessons on our financial journey was one I learned as our family was homeless for several months. At the time, I was pregnant with child number four and learning that God *delights* in giving good gifts. This simple revelation started to free me from the bondage of a poverty mentality. The summer when we had no permanent home, due to a rental deal falling through the day we were moving in, could have been wrought with anxiety and disappointment. But, instead, to this day we talk about this experience as one of the best summers of our lives, full of adventure and fun!

While waiting for clarity on what God had in mind for us, we left Bermuda, where we lived at the time, to borrow a flat of a relative in Philadelphia. From there, we travelled to many new places in America. We visited friends, went to a life-changing conference, and simply explored and enjoyed new places, all the while learning much about the goodness and faithfulness of God. Now, ten years later we live in one of the locations God brought us to that summer. Had we not been there then, learning about His ability to provide, we may not have had the faith to take the big risk it required to relocate.

Men and women tend to struggle with the area of finance from different perspectives. Women seem to equate financial stability with feeling *safe*. However, there is no safer place to look for financial security than in God. Your husband may be a great, or not so great, provider, but he is not *the* Provider! God is our first husband, and the source of every good gift. Unlike our earthly husbands, He cannot ever run out of energy or resources. I am learning to ask God for *all* my desires; from the simplest whimsical wishes, to the big needs of our family of ten. He loves to give good gifts to His children!

> *"For your Maker is your husband—*
> *the LORD Almighty is his name—*
> *the Holy One of Israel is your Redeemer;*
> *he is called the God of all the earth."* (Isaiah 54:5)

> *"Every good and perfect gift is from above,*
> *coming down from the Father of the heavenly lights,*
> *who does not change like shifting shadows."*
> **(James 1:17)**

For men, financial stability seemingly represents a sense of being *in control*. Being able to provide for their family makes them feel like capable and dependable men. It's a given that men should work hard to provide for their families. But if in doing so they depend on their own ability, above trusting God, self-sufficiency can become an idol. It doesn't make one less of a man when one surrenders the ultimate financial responsibility to God. Quite the contrary, trusting God as the perfect Provider makes one a man of God!

> *"Abraham believed God,*
> *and it was credited to him as righteousness,*
> *and he was called God's friend."* (James 2:23)

> *"No one can serve two masters.*
> *Either he will hate the one and love the other,*
> *or he will be devoted to the one and despise the other.*
> *You cannot serve both God and Money."* (Matthew 6:24)

I admit that our family still has a lot to learn about money. But when worry loses its sting, and trust increases as God proves His faithfulness, growing in financial stewardship becomes much easier. Although we are affected by the world we live in, we are not limited to its resources and strategies. I suspect that we have barely scratched the surface of how God will provide supernaturally for His children in the days to come. Just as in so many other areas where common paradigms and culture influence us, the battle ground largely is the mind. So, as people of faith, let's settle in our minds that God can provide for *all* that He asks us to both do and be.

> *"We take captive every thought*
> *to make it obedient to Christ."* (2 Corinthians 10:5)

> *"Do not conform to the pattern of this world,*
> *but be transformed by the renewing of your mind.*
> *Then you will be able to test and approve*
> *what God's will is—*
> *his good, pleasing and perfect will."* (Romans 12:2)

If you have been disappointed in your walk with God concerning financial provision, I encourage you to trust Him again. God is not a vending machine or Santa Claus. When we ask Him for something, we must ask with a surrendered heart. We need to want His *perfect will* for us more than "we want what we want". Also, we must not allow our experiences and circumstances to dictate truth. If God's Word says something and we don't see it manifest yet, we can be sure that it's not because God is wrong. The issue normally deals with timing, and a testing of our faith. We also do well to remember that tithing and giving generously are major keys to blessing. We are never too poor to give.

> *"Give and it will be given to you. A good measure,*
> *pressed down shaken together and running over,*
> *will be poured into your lap."* (Luke 6:38)

"'Bring the whole tithe into the storehouse,
that there may be food in my house.
Test me in this,' says the Lord Almighty,
'and see if I will not throw open the floodgates of heaven
and pour out so much blessing
that there will not be room enough to store it.'" (Malachi 3:10)

In our family we generally don't ask *people* for what we need, we ask God. If others are meant to be involved in our provision we find that God impresses them thus. We are commanded to become like little children in our trust in Abba. After all, isn't that what life with Him is about; learning that He indeed is a trustworthy Father!

So many people live a limited version of their best adventure, because they believe that finances can dictate their destiny. God supernaturally provided for thousands of His Israelite children in the desert for 40 years. Surely, He can provide for all the little ones He wants to give our families. Remember, He loves our children more than we ever could. And if there are areas where He calls us to sacrifice, let's do it gladly, knowing that our reward will be great.

"Behold, I am coming quickly,
and My reward is with Me,
to render to every man according to what
he has done." (Revelation 22:12)

Reasoning Three: "I can't have more children because I'm still too broken/messed-up/insecure. My marriage is still too new/fragile/unhealthy"

When I was surprised by my first pregnancy, only one month after our wedding, I was a mess, and so was my marriage. I was needy, co-dependent, and in great need of inner healing. The question I ask myself now is: Would I have grown, healed, and matured faster if I had more time to focus on my own needs and marriage before I had a child? The conclusion I come to is; most likely not.

Was it hard to become a parent while still immature and struggling? Yes. But again, pain is many times what gives us motivation to deal with things. I remember signing up for a course on anger management because I didn't want my children to suffer from my pent-up, unresolved hurt from the past. The fact that my children were there, as I faced my own dysfunction, became motivation for me to heal and learn quickly. Not having children certainly makes it easier to give up, both on ourselves and our marriage.

I know people who were told by not so gentle friends that they should have stopped having children due to the dysfunction of their family. Well, I guess if God would put those well-meaning friends in charge of wombs many more would remain closed. When is a person mature enough to become a parent, and who makes that decision? As Adam and Eve plunged the whole planet into sin, God still allowed them to birth new life. He didn't put the order of creation on pause until the sin issue was dealt with.

Let's also consider Abraham and Sarah. Were they mature enough, even at their old age, where we would choose them as parents of God's people? Was their marriage healthy? (You can read their story of doubt, lying, and big mistakes in Genesis 12-20.) Or what about David, fathering the wisest King ever known through the act of adultery? The list of dysfunctional people parenting amazing children goes on throughout history. Is it outrageous? Yes. Does it go against our logical way of thinking? Yes. But then again, God has been known to offend multitudes of people through the ages.

No matter the dysfunctional situation in which a child may be conceived, born, and raised, God has the ability to turn ashes into gold. My firstborn sadly suffered from our immaturity more than the later children, but she also served as motivation for us to grow as individuals and a family unit. The Lord promises that "where sin abounds grace abounds much more" (Romans 5:20). His "power is made perfect in weakness" (2 Corinthians 12:9).

Now Ronya, our firstborn, is 18 and is cultivating a strong character and love for the Lord. The gold that we see in her was unearthed through some difficult experiences. Some of them due to her imperfect parents, and some due to her own life choices. It is natural for us to want to protect our children from painful things. But in the midst of imperfection we need to trust in the One who can transform struggles into strength.

Let's briefly address the struggle that may arise when one spouse is further along in surrendering a family decision than the other. In the apparent disunity of the situation, it may feel like we face two God-given commands that clash in our lives. As women, we are counseled not only to bear children, but to respect and honor our husbands (Ephesians 5:24). What is a woman to do when her husband does not agree to let God hold the keys to the womb? Well, I am certain that obedience to God, based on rebellion towards our husband, is not obedience at all. If you are in a situation where you desire full surrender, and your husband doesn't, all I can advise you to do is *pray*.

Prayer is the single most powerful weapon for the change of someone's heart. I hear many success stories of God answering such prayers. Manipulation and control won't accomplish the desired unity, only prayer will. The main thing for a woman (or man if the situation is reversed) in this predicament, is to make sure that her (or his) own heart stays pure before God. The Lord sees our desires and willingness to obey, and rewards us accordingly. He is also very good at redeeming things that are seemingly lost. You may still have your designated number of children, although starting at a later time.

Even after my husband and I both became convicted that the Lord wanted our surrender and trust regarding the womb, there were still times of questions and struggle in the process. My husband admits that relinquishing control in the area of family planning was not a one time event, but a continuous journey, as children were added to our family. We were not always in perfect unity and sync with each other during this process, but the Lord was always faithful in bringing us to such a place. Extending grace to our spouse and being patient is important, as full surrender may come in stages.

Before concluding this section, I want to give attention to those who struggle with the idea of more children due to physical, rather than emotional or relational, difficulties. With heartache, I have observed friends with severely traumatic pregnancies and births. The devil uses such foul tactics to prevent God's chosen from being born. It's understandable why these attacks deter families from having more children. I have also seen those who, with fierce determination, faith, and courage, press through and surrender their womb to God yet again, knowing they may go through real physical suffering. I believe there are special rewards for these brave ones!

Reasoning Four: "If I had many children, I couldn't pursue my career/fulfill God's call on my life. I would need to give up too much"

I was excited to learn a while ago that the anti-aging hormone "estriol" increases 1000 times in our bodies during pregnancy![33] I sometimes hear talk about pregnancy as something that robs and depletes women. This is a very partial truth. Babies certainly benefit from the mother's supply of

---

[33]https://www.avawomen.com/avaworld/hormones-101/

many good things, but God makes sure she is greatly rewarded for the sacrifice. I am amazed by many moms of big families who look beautiful, fit, healthy, and vibrant. Personally, I have racked up a deposit of 72 months of boosted anti-aging hormones. I would love to have a look inside my cells. I plan on cashing in on all that good stuff and stay healthy and strong for a very long time.

Research shows that when we allow our bodies to work according to their God-given cycles, without disturbing the hormonal balance, we increase our chance of staying healthy many times over. I believe this is an area where the principle applies that when we put God's Kingdom *first*, all other things are given to us (Matthew 6:33). The Lord also promises that when we keep His commands, He places none of the sicknesses of Egypt on us (Exodus 15:26). Following is a quote from one of the many studies confirming the protection God built into the lifecycle of the female body:

> *Recent studies report that pregnancy produces a protective effect against breast and ovarian cancers. The more pregnancies you go through — and the younger you start having babies — the greater the effect; some research has found that breastfeeding for more than three months can also lower the risk of certain cancers.*[34]

Now, let's get to the point of why I am sharing this. I remember many years ago, sitting on a swing in a playground, watching my children play. I

---

[34]http://health.howstuffworks.com/pregnancy-and-parenting/pregnancy/issues/six-surprising-benefits-of-pregnancy4.htm

was in deep thought, wondering when I would get expression for other gifts and the creativity God had placed in me. At that moment, I heard the Lord's whisper. He told me that my more active and productive years outside the home would *start* in my 40's. He didn't say it would never happen. He just turned the current societal model of life up-side-down.

In the West, we delay childbirth until it's almost too late, in order to pursue careers first. But the created lifecycle of the female body says that our twenties, thirties, and perhaps even forties, are child-bearing years. The pregnancies during this time are designed to bless our bodies to be healthy and active, even after our children are grown. Imagine the wisdom and experience we gain as we spend years of our lives raising people from infancy to mature adulthood. If we do things God's way, the world not only benefits from our growth through this process, but receives a generation of children parented by truly present adults.

For women who carry a strong desire to be in the marketplace, I understand that the natural lifecycle can look like a threat. We may be less desired in certain professions as we get older. I just plead with you not to limit what God can do. Dare to surrender your desires to Him. He is so creative, and cares about us so deeply. Let's trust Him with the very gifts, passions, and abilities that He Himself placed within us. And let's remember, that our womb is one of those gifts!

"Now to him who is able to do immeasurably more than all we ask or imagine,

according to his power that is at work within us..."
(Ephesians 3:20)

As women, we have more to offer the world than giving it our children, even though that certainly is enough of a gift! The woman described in Proverbs 31 clearly proves that women possess a wealth of contribution to render. The Bible describes that she offers the world her children, supports her husband, and blesses the world with her business ventures, investments, creativity, and charity, as well as provides employment for others. She doesn't do these feats as a tired, grumpy, worn out woman, but one full of confidence and strength.

The Proverbs 31 woman didn't have to choose between home-making, career and ministry. She got to do all of it and do it with excellence! I know women who dislike the very thought of the Proverbs 31 woman, because they feel she represents an unrealistic ideal, impossible to live up to. I don't see the description of her life as a measuring rod. I see this woman, who says to be worth more than rubies, as an inspiration to trust what *God* can accomplish through a surrendered life. Let's read about her with our faith-lenses on and dare to dream.

"A wife of noble character who can find?
She is worth far more than rubies.
Her husband has full confidence in her
and lacks nothing of value.
She brings him good, not harm, all the days of her life.

She selects wool and flax and works with eager hands.

She is like the merchant ships,

bringing her food from afar.

She gets up while it is still night;

she provides food for her family

and portions for her female servants.

She considers a field and buys it;

out of her earnings she plants a vineyard.

She sets about her work vigorously;

her arms are strong for her tasks.

She sees that her trading is profitable,

and her lamp does not go out at night.

In her hand she holds the distaff

and grasps the spindle with her fingers.

She opens her arms to the poor

and extends her hands to the needy.

When it snows, she has no fear for her household;

for all of them are clothed in scarlet.

She makes coverings for her bed;

she is clothed in fine linen and purple.

Her husband is respected at the city gate,

where he takes his seat among the elders of the land.

She makes linen garments and sells them,

and supplies the merchants with sashes.

She is clothed with strength and dignity;

she can laugh at the days to come.

She speaks with wisdom,

and faithful instruction is on her tongue.

She watches over the affairs of her household

and does not eat the bread of idleness.

Her children arise and call her blessed;

her husband also, and he praises her:

'Many women do noble things,

but you surpass them all.'

Charm is deceptive, and beauty is fleeting;

but a woman who fears the LORD is to be praised.

Honor her for all that her hands have done,

and let her works bring her praise at the city gate."

(Proverbs 31:10-31)

If God guides our schedule, we can have seasons of much activity, accompanied by favor to make it enjoyable. I inadvertently miss His direction at times, trying to accomplish too much in my own strength. At these times there is no favor, only stress and frustration. Because of this the children, my marriage, and home suffer. I am NOT advocating mothers being involved in all kinds of "doing" outside the home. If we ever get too busy to prioritize raising our own children, we are simply too busy. Jesus had no problem postponing the care of the many needy grown-ups, to spend time loving on children (Mark 10:14).

I am illustrating, however, that it is *possible* with God to be in seasons of great creativity and productivity, even during child-bearing years. Now, in my early 40's, I am much busier than when I sat in that play-ground years ago, wondering when I would get to express my other passions. I'm not even sure how it all happened; a CD-project, publishing books, training young worshippers and musicians etc. I'm telling God that if this is what I get to do while still in my child-bearing age, I can't imagine what comes later. Whatever *He* has us do in each particular period of life will flow out of us as naturally as living water. In fact, I am convinced that only with our seasons surrendered to God will we ever express the fullness of what He placed within us.

*"The water I give them will become in them
a spring of water welling up to eternal life."*
(John 4:14)

*"Come to me, all you who are weary and burdened,
and I will give you rest.
Take my yoke upon you and learn from me,
for I am gentle and humble in heart,
and you will find rest for your souls.
For my yoke is easy and my burden is light."*
(Matthew 11:28-30)

*"If anyone does not know
how to manage his own family,
how can he take care of God's church?"*
(1 Timothy 3:4-5)

QUESTIONS

1. Can you recognize any of the fears/thinking patterns in your own mind from this chapter, related to larger families? If yes, which ones?

2. Can you think of additional fears that arise in you as you consider surrendering your womb to God? What are they?

3. What truths in God's Word speak to the fears you recognize within yourself?

CONCLUSION

As I was getting ready to write the conclusion of this book, the Lord reminded me of when I was a little girl, singing a song from *The Sound of Music*. I saw myself again, barefoot on that stage, confidently blasting out: *"A captain with seven children, what's so fearsome about that?!"* I can imagine the Lord laughing then, as He looked into my future!

There are days I question God on His decision to make me a mother of a large family. If I were to choose someone to raise mighty men and women of God, I would not choose me. There are days when I feel like a failure in the very thing I encourage others to do. I remind myself that it is by His *grace* that we fulfill any and every calling on our lives. If Jesus learned obedience through the things He suffered, perhaps the hard days are a gift for me as well. Without Him I can do nothing, but with Him all things are possible!

"Unless the LORD builds the house, its builders labor in vain." (Psalm 127:1)

I believe that, as more of God's people are reintroduced to the significance of the womb, many will choose to surrender their family planning to Him. I can't wait for a generation of women in particular, to find *peace* in the role God designed for them. I can't wait for them to dare to question the "New Normal" in society and take back the beauty the enemy robbed from motherhood. May women discover that mothering and homemaking is not a narrow role, but one full of exciting possibilities. It is not a cookie cutter reality, but one that God tailors differently for each family, with their unique parenting style, passions, and gifts.

A few years ago, the night before my husband's birthday, I sat down to make him a home-made card. I prayed that God's Spirit would guide me. I opened a secular magazine to find a picture to cut out for the front, and on the first page was a man running on top of water. I immediately cut it out for his card. When I started writing the birthday greeting, a statement popped into my spirit: *"Safe is not as fun!"* I knew that God, once again, was challenging him, and our family, to step out of the boat unto the water. Our best adventure is always one journeyed by faith, not by sight.

We are at big cross-roads as a family right now. As all families, we have hard choices to make. In our faith walk it can seem like we constantly choose between safety and risk, but the choice is really between safety and *fun*. There is so much we miss out on if we choose a "safe life". There are countless adventures, celebrations, and lessons we miss if we do things our way. Which, by the way, really doesn't ensure safety anyway. Real safety only lies in the seemingly "scary" adventure with God. It is a paradox, I know, but then again, God is full of those!

From a prophetic perspective, the message in this book is not without urgency. We live in a time when many things are shaken and tested. True surrender in such times is crucial to our continued journey with God. I'm convinced that God's plans for these times to a large degree depend on our response of obedience to all He asks of us. If indeed a generation needs to be born and raised to prepare the way for His Kingdom, then we do well to allow them entry. May we truly see that we are part of a bigger picture and that the decisions we make concerning our womb affect the destiny of *nations and generations.* Selfish gain and desires have no place in radical discipleship and Kingdom mentality.

If the only thing you get out of reading my story is a determination to ensure your heart is surrendered to God, I am excited. If you purpose to ask His opinion on your womb and family planning, I am thrilled. If you dare to face your fears and step out of the boat, despite the waves on the water, you have made my efforts so worthwhile. Thank you for giving me your ear and attention. Now, Holy Spirit, the rest is up to you!

APPENDIX I

A CLOSED, WEAK, OR DEPRIVED WOMB

Reading a book like this must be hard for anyone who has been told they can't conceive. It breaks my heart to meet people who are in touch with their God-given desire to become a parent, but who remain barren no matter how hard they try. I want to share with you that I have faith for the healing and opening of wombs. If you haven't already reviewed the stories in the Bible where God opens closed wombs, I encourage you to do so to stir up faith for your own miracle. Also, there are countless present-day testimonies to encourage you.

Following is a list of possible reasons why a womb may be barren:

1. God closes a womb temporarily, and looks for our surrender and trust in His perfect timing. Remember, even after Abraham and Sarah had received their promise of a son at their old age, their faith was tested while waiting for the manifestation.

2. A consequence of our own manipulation of the hormonal balance in our body through the use of contraceptives. In this case, repentance and prayer for healing can restore balance.

3. Conditions in this world that are partially outside of our control which influence our bodies negatively; such as pollution, stress,

hormone disturbing chemicals found in foods etc. For these things we can also pray for healing and protection.

4. Generational curses, whether physical or spiritual, passed down through family lines. There is great power in Jesus' blood as we take authority to break off all such limiting factors.

5. Word curses and doubt that we ourselves, or others, have spoken over us. These word curses need to be cancelled in prayer, and declaration of truth spoken in their place.

6. Sinful behavior that hinder God's blessings from flowing to us. Repentance is the key.

7. Lastly, in a truly surrendered life we may need to ask God if a childless life is part of His calling for us. This is similar to someone being called to live as a single person to fulfill their life mission, even though God designed us for marriage (1 Corinthians 7).

Following is a prayer that you can pray if you have a closed womb. I also encourage you to write your own prayers, using Scriptures that speak to you personally. Pray these prayers consistently, until breakthrough comes. God loves to open wombs and loves the fruit of the womb. He loves to heal and restore. He IS the very Source of Life! He is full of grace and mercy and is the giver of good and perfect gifts. In Him, hope is always alive!

DAILY PRAYER FOR AN OPEN WOMB

Father,

I come to present my request to You for a healthy, open, and receptive womb, and I do so with thanksgiving (Philippians 4:6). I thank You for everything You have already done and given to me in my life. I thank You that Your plans for my future are good (Jeremiah 29:11). Even though I don't always understand Your ways, or Your timing, I choose to trust You (Psalm 9:10). I thankfully confess that I believe that You are never late, and that Your ways are perfect (Isaiah 55:9).

Holy Spirit, I pray that You search my heart to show me if there is any offensive way in me (Psalm 139:23-24). If there is any judgment, jealousy, bitterness, or un-forgiveness in my heart towards anybody, I confess it and ask for Your forgiveness (Matthew 6:14). If there is any un-surrendered part of my life and heart, I confess it and ask that You forgive me. I surrender to You and receive Your forgiveness and cleansing (1 John 1:9).

I thank You Jesus, that because of Your sacrifice for me there is nothing that can hinder Your will in my life (Romans 8:37). I plead the mighty blood of Your death, and power of Your resurrection, over myself! I cancel any generational curse from my father's, mother's, or in-laws' side, causing a closed or weak womb, in Your name. In its place, I receive the blessing of a fruitful womb from You. As it is in heaven, let it be in my body (Matthew 6:10)!

If there have been any word curses spoken over me, my husband, or family, I declare them failed and made null and void in Your name (Galatians 3:13). In the place of negative words, I receive Your truth which accomplishes what it is sent to do and does not fail (Isaiah 55:11). I declare that You who started a good work in me will complete it (Philippians 1:6). I declare that what You have in store for me is beyond my wildest dreams (1 Corinthians 2:9). I declare that nothing is impossible with You, and that I can do all things through You (Matthew 19:26).

Now Father God, I receive Your peace that passes all understanding and go on living in Your rest (Philippians 4:7). Thank You for always being faithful to me (1 Corinthians 10:13). Thank You that Your grace towards me is new each day (Lamentations 3:22-23). Thank You that nothing can take away Your love for me (Romans 8:39). May I grow to be a parent like You, as I raise the fruit of my womb to come! In Jesus' name, Amen.

APPENDIX II
BEYOND ABORTION

Diana's story

I was 18 years old and had kept my vow that I would not have sex before this age. Even though I was not a believer I was quite strong-willed and felt no need to follow the crowd – growing up it was quite normal for many girls to be sexually active as early as 12. You were certainly expected to have lost your virginity by the age of 16! Now, at 18, I was with what I considered to be my first 'real' boyfriend whom I really liked. Although I still didn't feel ready to go all the way I allowed it to happen. That decision changed everything.

We were being what is considered responsible, we used protection... but it didn't work! As a result, my very first time with a man I got pregnant. Although I skipped my period I didn't do a pregnancy test for months as I was in complete denial. Finally, after constant persuasion from my then best friend, I took the test. Even though logically I knew what the result would be, I was still in shock to see the results.

Before becoming pregnant, if you asked me where I stood concerning the topic of abortion, I would have been against it. It wasn't a strong conviction, but I just thought it was wrong. When my friend continually advised me to make an appointment to see a doctor and get a date for an abortion before it was too late, it took me a while to even consider it.

Eventually I went on the premise that I didn't have to go through with it, it just gave me the option, which by now began to look like a good option – it would clear up the mess I was in. However, as part of the procedure I needed to go and have an ultrasound. As I saw the life growing on the ultrasound screen I started to question whether I could follow through with the procedure. Shortly after this I decided in my heart that I was going to keep the baby.

During these months the only person that knew I was pregnant was my friend. I had not told the father as we had not long ago ended our relationship. Although I really wanted to tell my mother I hadn't yet, since every time I went to tell her it seemed like the wrong moment. Two days before the scheduled procedure I finally gathered up the courage to talk to her. She was not angry but sad that I hadn't told her earlier. She felt it would not be good for me or the baby to go through with the pregnancy, and strongly advised me not to. She was the person I trusted most in life and somehow, I allowed her conviction to override my own.

I called the child's father to tell him the news. He told me he was absolutely not ready to be a father and offered to come with me to the clinic the next day. As we went to have the procedure performed, it felt as if I was having an out-of-body-experience; as if I wasn't really present in what was happening. It was as if I went to this place for an abstract reason; was put to sleep, woke up and went home with bad period pains. It was extremely surreal.

Due to strong denial I didn't face what had happened until much later. It all came crashing down on me just before Christmas. I reached down to rub my belly as I had gotten in the habit of doing while pregnant. All of a sudden, I realized that nothing was there because I had killed my baby! I kept thinking 'What have I done!' I was faced with the reality that I could never reverse things or take it back. It was like waking up to a nightmare.

I was alone with my feelings for a long time. Everyone seemed to talk about abortion in such a casual way, as if it was a normal thing to do, and I thought something was wrong with me. I did my best to suppress the guilt, shame, mourning and sense of loss and simply go on with life. But something had happened inside of me. My self-worth and self- esteem became very low. This in turn led me to make some poor decisions. I did things that were completely out of character and got into a destructive and abusive relationship. Several other similar relationships were to follow.

I now know these actions were a direct result of my guilt, thinking less of myself and a form of self-punishment for what I had done. Starting at the age of 21, I suffered from progressively worsening depression and insomnia. At first, I could manage the depression by staying busy, working or studying. But suddenly, a few years later I couldn't manage to hold up this mask any longer. I became suddenly tearful and emotional without being able to control myself and started to retreat and isolate. These times of break-down would reoccur and I would often be filled with hatred for myself and suicidal thoughts.

Although I was without my child, I felt like I had a ghost growing up with me. Every year at the time my baby would have been born I would think about how old he/she would be. I would see other children the age of mine and constantly be reminded of what I had done. Even as I was able to start talking about these things many years later, I could never do so without crying.

Finally, at the age of 27, as I was at an all-time low, I was alone in my apartment and cried out to God. I told Him that if He did exist, I could not do life on my own any longer. The experience that followed cannot be explained with words. I felt an immediate lifting of the depression. I felt heat come through my whole body working its way up. Everything was fine and wonderful in an instant. I knew that God was real!

A couple of days later the cousin of a friend of mine started to tell me about Jesus. He explained that He had died for my sins and that if I would accept it, I could be forgiven. I remember knowing that what he was saying was truth, although I was normally a very logical person wanting proof. As I questioned what I was being told, the Holy Spirit let me know what I was hearing was right. I remember thinking 'Wow, how could You forgive me for killing my own child, God?!' It blew me away. I kept thinking that God must really love me a lot.

Through my journey as a believer I understood that everything I had secretly felt as the record played over and over in my mind that I had killed my own child, was true. From psalm 139 I understood that I wasn't crazy after all for feeling so strongly about ending a life in the womb. It was murder. It was a life taken. It was a child, my child. It was the world that was lying. My feelings about abortion were correct. The fact that my guilt was validated made the forgiveness all the more meaningful.

Although I did receive God's forgiveness and experienced a radical lifting of the depression, it was a process for me to forgive myself and receive all my healing. One thing that really helped with this was a counseling group for mothers who had had abortions, led by a believer, which a friend introduced me to. Going there helped me to learn to talk in depth about the reality of my experience.

I learned that it is important to take the time to really grieve. I learned to fully take responsibility for my choice and to forgive anyone who had influenced me that I had secretly blamed, especially my mom who was also a believer by now.   For years my relationship with my mom had been affected by the resentment and anger that I had harbored against her. Confessing this to her was huge for me. Finally, I could fully forgive her and also myself.

One thing I realized while meeting many other women in my situation in that group was that the abortion had affected them all deeply. Some were not believers and were adamant about the fact that they had done no wrong, but still, for some reason, they needed counseling. Something deep inside of all of them, behind all the denial, knew that it was terribly wrong. It also became apparent that the very symptoms that I had had; the depression, insomnia, destructive relationships and living with a ghost child, were things that many of them suffered from as well.

Sometimes when we have aborted a child, we can subconsciously believe that we will never have or deserve another one. For me getting married and then having a daughter, almost at the exact time of year that I would have given birth had I kept my first child, was very healing for me. Today as I talk about my experience I can do so without tears. I will never forget what happened, but God healed me from the pain of the event. I'm not depressed anymore, and I don't live with guilt. It is so freeing to know that my child is with God, and until I get to meet him/her I can live in the state of being forgiven!

-Diana

OTHER MATERIALS BY MIA WHITE

Books:

30 Day Poet: Feed your writer's bug (2018)

Beautifully Born: Empowering women for natural birth (2019)

Music:

A Pure Heart (2012)

Beloved (2019)

You Tube:

Music video *Gift of a Child* by Mia Talita (2012)

Conversations on Natural Birth, teaching series (2019)

Made in the USA
Middletown, DE
24 January 2023

22422404R00070